Meno

Plato

Meno

Translated by
G.M.A. GRUBE

HACKETT PUBLISHING COMPANY, INC.
Indianapolis • Cambridge

Cover design by Richard L. Listenberger

ISBN-13: 978-0-915144-24-2
ISBN-10: 0-915144-24-7

Library of Congress Catalog Card Number: 76-40412

19 18 17 16 15   15 16 17 18 19

For further information, address Hackett Publishing Co., Inc.,
Box 44937, Indianapolis, Indiana 46244-0937
www.hackettpublishing.com

Printed in the United States of America

CONTENTS

G.M.A. GRUBE and the publisher acknowledge with appreciation the extensive help of Richard Hogan and Donald J. Zeyl in correcting and improving this second edition of the *Meno*.

INTRODUCTION

The *Meno* is one of the earlier Platonic dialogues, the so-called Socratic, which seek to define ethical terms, in this case virtue, and fail to find a satisfactory definition. We cannot date it exactly; it is probably not one of the very earliest, but it is clearly written before the *Phaedo* as well as the *Republic*. We shall probably not be far wrong if we date it about 390 B.C. or very shortly after. On the other hand, the supposed date of the imaginary conversation can be fixed within narrow limits: Anytus, who takes part in the conversation, was a successful democratic politician in Athens (see 90a–b), and his success must have come after the restoration of democratic government in Athens in 403 B.C., whereas Meno himself joined the expedition of Cyrus, described by Xenophon in the *Anabasis*, in 401 and never came back to Greece. So the conversation must be imagined to have taken place between those two dates, say in 402. We know from the *Apology* that Anytus was one of Socrates' accusers in 399, and Plato obviously expects his readers to have this in mind.

Meno is mentioned several times in the *Anabasis*, and Xenophon gives him a most unpleasant character (II, 6, 21 ff.): Greedy for wealth and power, ambitious, a treacherous friend always seeking his own advantage in everything, "He thought that the quickest way to achieve what he wanted was through perjury, lies and deceit; simplicity and truthfulness were to him merely silly . . . he secured the obedience of his men by joining in their misdeeds," and more in the same vein. Meno's character is not immediately relevant to the discussion, but Plato seems to expect his readers to know of his reputation, for this knowledge adds something to the bitter irony of certain statements made by and about him, "the hereditary friend of the Great King."

The dialogue makes a good introduction to Plato, for the subjects discussed frequently reappear in later dialogues, and some of them are basic to the Socratic-Platonic philosophy. They are here fully explained. In the first part of the dialogue Socrates is at some pains to make Meno understand the nature of a general definition and to correct the logical mistakes the latter makes, such as failing to understand the difference between a definition and an enumeration of particular examples, or including the term to be defined in the definition. The theory that all learning is recollection of knowledge

1

innate in the soul, which assumes the immortality of the soul, and also the theory of Forms (though the latter is not here mentioned) will reappear in the *Phaedo* and the *Phaedrus*. That virtue is a kind of knowledge is an essential part of Socratic thinking, yet the theory is here discussed with arguments pro and con and is left an open question at the end. The introduction of true opinion or belief as a guide to right conduct is important in the *Republic* and other Platonic works. The examination of Meno's slave explicitly illustrates the various steps of the Socratic examination or *elenchus*. The elimination of the kind of ignorance that believes it knows constitutes always the first step in Platonic education. Anytus' vehement dislike of the Sophists should also be noted, for Plato disliked them as much from first to last, if for different reasons. The democratic politician presumably disliked them because their followers would be the rich and idle young men, and he suspected them accordingly, whereas Plato disliked their teaching because it was superficial, aimed at worldly success, and had little regard for the truth. He disliked rhetoric — which they all taught — for the same reasons.

NOTE: Except in rare instances, the translation follows Burnet's Oxford text. The only liberty taken is where the answers to Socrates' questions are very brief, merely indicating assent or the like. In such instances I have replaced the initial "M" by a dash to indicate change of speaker.

70 - 71

theme: virtue - how it's acquired
- nature v. nurture of a "man"

• Gorgia
• Sophists

• admired for wealth, now
  wisdom → different in Athens
       ↳ not as valued ⟶

• Socrates dig @ Meno's teach. from Gor
  - Being an expert in any
    fied (70b-c)

• dearth - lack

MENO

MENO: Can you tell me, Socrates, can virtue1 be taught? Or is it not teachable but the result of practice, or is it neither of these, but men possess it by nature or in some other way?   70

SOCRATES: Before now, Meno, Thessalians had a high reputation among the Greeks and were admired for their horsemanship and their wealth, but now, it seems to me, they are also admired for their wisdom,   b
not least the fellow citizens of your friend Aristippus of Larissa. The responsibility for this reputation of yours lies with Gorgias,[2] for when he came to your city he found that the leading Aleuadae, your lover Aristippus among them, loved him for his wisdom, and so did the other leading Thessalians. In particular, he accustomed you to give a bold and grand answer to any question you may be asked, as experts are likely to do. Indeed, he himself   c
was ready to answer any Greek who wished to question him, and every question was answered. But here in Athens, my dear Meno, the opposite is the case, as if there were a dearth of wisdom, and wisdom seems to have departed hence to go to you. If then you want to ask one of us that sort of   71
question, everyone will laugh and say: "Good stranger, you must think me happy indeed if you think I know whether virtue can be taught or how it comes to be; I am so far from knowing whether virtue can be taught or not that I do not even have any knowledge of what virtue itself is."

---

1. The Greek word is *aretê*. It can refer to specific virtues such as moderation, courage et cetera, but it is also used for *the* virtue or conglomeration of virtues that makes a man virtuous or good. In this dialogue it is mostly used in this more general sense. Socrates himself at times (e.g., 93 b ff.) uses "good" as equivalent to virtuous.

2. Gorgias was perhaps the most famous of the earlier generation of Sophists, those traveling teachers who arose in the late fifth century to fill the need for higher education. They all taught rhetoric, or the art of speaking, but as Meno tells us, Gorgias concenrtated on this more than the others and made fewer general claims for his teaching (95c). He visited Athens in 427 B.C., and his rhetorical devices gave him an immediate success. Plato named one of his dialogues after him. Fairly substantive fragments of his writings are extant.

3

b   I myself, M[eno] ... r, and I
blame myself ... ot know
what somethi[ng] ... do you
think that so[me] ... d know
whether he is ... of these?
Do you think

M: I do n[ot] ... e is? Are
c   we to report t[o] ...

S: Not o[nly] ... ever yet
met anyone e[lse] ...

M: How s[o]

S: I did.

M: Did y[ou]

S: I do n[ot] ... you now
what I thoug[ht] ... d to say,
d   so you remin[d] ... willing,
for surely you

S: Let us ... o, by the
gods, what do you yourself say that virtue is? Speak and do not begrudge us,
so that I may have spoken a most unfortunate untruth when I said that I
had never met anyone who knew, if you and Gorgias are shown to know.

e   M: It is not hard to tell you, Socrates. First, if you want the virtue of a
man, it is easy to say that a man's virtue consists of being able to manage
public affairs and in so doing to benefit his friends and harm his enemies
and to be careful that no harm comes to himself; if you want the virtue of a
woman, it is not difficult to describe: she must manage the home well, pre-
serve its possessions, and be submissive to her husband; the virtue of a child,
whether male or female, is different again, and so is that of an elderly man,
if you want that, or if you want that of a free man or a slave. And there are
72   very many other virtues, so that one is not at a loss to say what virtue is.
There is virtue for every action and every age, for every task of ours and
every one of us—and Socrates, the same is true for wickedness.

S: I seem to be in great luck, Meno; while I am looking for one virtue, I
have found you to have a whole swarm of them. But, Meno, to follow up the
b   image of swarms, if I were asking you what is the nature of bees, and you
said that they are many and of all kinds, what would you answer if I asked
you: "Do you mean that they are many and varied and different from one
another in so far as they are bees? Or are they no different in that regard, but
in some other respect, in their beauty, for example, or their size or in some
other such way?" Tell me, what would you answer if thus questioned?

M: I would say that they do not differ from one another in being bees.

Handwritten notes:

- knowing of virtue
  - Socrates does not know
  - Meno does
- multiple virtues
  - Socrates looking for 1
  - (72 C) have same form to make them virtues
- Comparing health of man + woman to forms of virtue
- all relating to democracy in Greece? How?

S: If I went on to say: "Tell me, what is this very thing, Meno, in which   c
they are all the same and do not differ from one another?" Would you be
able to tell me?

M: I would.

S: The same is true in the case of the virtues. Even if they are many and
various, all of them have one and the same form[3] which makes them virtues,
and it is right to look to this when one is asked to make clear what virtue is.
Or do you not understand what I mean?   d

M: I think I understand, but I certainly do not grasp the meaning of the
question as fully as I want to.

S: I am asking whether you think it is only in the case of virtue that
there is one for man, another for woman and so on, or is the same true in the
case of health and size and strength? Do you think that there is one health
for man and another for woman? Or, if it is health, does it have the same
form everywhere, whether in man or in anything else whatever?   e

M: The health of a man seems to me the same as that of a woman.

S: And so with size and strength? If a woman is strong, that strength
will be the same and have the same form, for by "the same" I mean that
strength is no different as far as being strength, whether in a man or a
woman. Or do you think there is a difference?

M: I do not think so.

S: And will there be any difference in the case of virtue, as far as being
virtue is concerned, whether it be in a child or an old man, in a woman or in   73
a man?

M: I think, Socrates, that somehow this is no longer like those other
cases.

S: How so? Did you not say that the virtue of a man consists of managing the city well,[4] and that of a woman of managing the household? — I did.

---

3. The Greek term is *eidos*, which Plato was to use for his separately existing eternal
Forms. Its common meaning is stature or appearance. Socrates felt that if we apply
the same name or epithet to a number of different things or actions, they must surely
have a common characteristic to justify the use of the same term. A definition is then
a description of this "form" or appearance, which it presents to the mind's eye. In the
earlier dialogues however, as here, this form is not thought of as having a separate
existence, but as immanent.

4. When discussing goodness or morality, social and political virtues would be more
immediately present to the Greek mind than they are to ours. In both Plato and Aris-
totle a good man is above all a good citizen, whereas the modern mind thinks of goodness mainly in more individual terms, such as sobriety or sexual morals. An extreme
example of this occurred in a contemporary judge's summation to the jury in the case
of a woman of loose sexual behaviour who was accused of murdering her husband.
He actually said: "This is a case of murder, not of morals. The morals of the accused
have nothing to do with it."

S: Is it possible to manage a city well, or a household, or anything else, while not managing it moderately and justly? — Certainly not.

b   S: Then if they manage justly and moderately, they must do so with justice and moderation? — Necessarily.

S: So both the man and the woman, if they are to be good, need the same things, justice and moderation. — So it seems.

S: What about a child and an old man? Can they possibly be good if they are intemperate and unjust? — Certainly not.

S: But if they are moderate and just? — Yes.

c   S: So all human beings are good in the same way, for they become good by acquiring the same qualities. — It seems so.

S: And they would not be good in the same way if they did not have the same virtue. — They certainly would not be.

S: Since then the virtue of all is the same, try to tell me and to remember what Gorgias, and you with him, said that that same thing is.

d   M: What else but to be able to rule over men, if you are seeking one description to fit them all.

S: That is indeed what I am seeking, but Meno, is virtue the same in the case of a child or a slave, namely, for them to be able to rule over a master, and do you think that he who rules is still a slave? — I do not think so at all, Socrates.

S: It is not likely, my good man. Consider this further point: you say that virtue is to be able to rule. Shall we not add to this *justly and not unjustly*?

M: I think so, Socrates, for justice is virtue.

e   S: Is it virtue, Meno, or a virtue? — What do you mean?

S: As with anything else. For example, if you wish, take roundness, about which I would say that it is a shape, but not simply that it is shape. I would not so speak of it because there are other shapes.

M: You are quite right. So I too say that not only justice is a virtue but there are many other virtues.

74   S: What are they? Tell me, as I could mention other shapes to you if you bade me do so, so do you mention other virtues.

M: I think courage is a virtue, and moderation, wisdom, and munificence, and very many others.

S: We are having the same trouble again, Meno, though in another way; we have found many virtues while looking for one, but we cannot find the one which covers all the others.

M: I cannot yet find, Socrates, what you are looking for, one virtue for them all, as in the other cases. **b**

S: That is likely, but I am eager, if I can, that we should make progress, for you understand that the same applies to everything. If someone asked you what I mentioned just now: "What is shape, Meno?" and you told him that it was roundness, and if then he said to you what I did: "Is roundness shape or a shape?" you would surely tell him that it is a shape? — I certainly would.

S: That would be because there are other shapes? — Yes. **c**

S: And if he asked you further what they were, you would tell him? — I would.

S: So too, if he asked you what colour is, and you said it is white, and your questioner interrupted you, "Is white colour or a colour?" you would say that it is a colour, because there are also other colours? — I would.

S: And if he bade you mention other colours, you would mention others that are no less colours than white is? — Yes. **d**

S: Then if he pursued the argument as I did and said: "We always arrive at the many; do not talk to me in that way, but since you call all these many by one name, and say that no one of them is not a shape even though they are opposites, tell me what this is which applies as much to the round as to the straight and which you call shape, as you say the round is as much a shape as the straight." Do you not say that? — I do. **e**

S: When you speak like that, do you assert that the round is no more round than it is straight, and that the straight is no more straight than it is round?

M: Certainly not, Socrates.

S: Yet you say that the round is no more a shape man the straight is, nor the one more than the other. — That is true.

S: What then is this to which the name shape applies? Try to tell me. If then you answered the man who was questioning about shape or colour: "I do not understand what you want, my man, nor what you mean," he would **75** probably wonder and say: "You do not understand that I am seeking that which is the same in all these cases?" Would you still have nothing to say, Meno, if one asked you: "What is this which applies to the round and the straight and the other things which you call shapes and which is the same in them all?" Try to say, that you may practise for your answer about virtue.

M: No, Socrates, but you tell me. **b**

S: Do you want me to do you this favour?

M: I certainly do.

S: And you will then be willing to tell me about virtue?

M: I will.

S: We must certainly press on. The subject is worth it.

M: It surely is.

S: Come then, let us try to tell you what shape is. See whether you will accept that it is this: Let us say that shape is that which alone of existing things always follows colour. Is that satisfactory to you, or do you look for it in some other way? I should be satisfied if you defined virtue in this way.

c

M: But that is foolish, Socrates.

S: How do you mean?

M: That shape, you say, always follows colour. Well then, if someone were to say that he did not know what colour is, but that he had the same difficulty as he had about shape, what do you think your answer would be?

S: A true one, surely, and if my questioner was one of those clever and disputatious debaters, I would say to him: "I have given my answer; if it is wrong, it is your job to refute it." Then, if they are friends as you and I are, and want to discuss with each other, they must answer in a manner more gentle and more proper to discussion. By this I mean that the answers must not only be true, but in terms admittedly known to the questioner. I too will try to speak in these terms. Do you call something "the end?" I mean such a thing as a limit or boundary, for all those are, I say, the same thing. Prodicus[5] might disagree with us, but you surely call something "finished" or "completed" — that is what I want to express, nothing elaborate.

d

e

M: I do, and I think I understand what you mean.

76

S: Further, you call something a plane, and something else a solid, as in geometry?

M: I do.

S: From this you may understand what I mean by shape, for I say this of every shape, that a shape is that which limits a solid; in a word, a shape is the limit of a solid.

M: And what do you say colour is, Socrates?

S: You are outrageous, Meno. You bother an old man to answer questions, but you yourself are not willing to recall and to tell me what Gorgias says that virtue is.

b

---

5. Prodicus was a well-known Sophist who was especially keen on the exact meaning of words, and he was fond of making the proper distinctions between words of similar but not identical meanings. We see him in action in the *Protagoras* of Plato (especially 337 a–c) where he apperas with two other distinguished Sophists, Protagoras and Hippias. His insistence on the proper definition of words would naturally endear him to Socrates who, in Plato, always treats him with more sympathy than he does the other Sophists. The point here is that Prodicus would object to "end," "limit," and "boundary" being treated as "all the same thing."

M: After you have answered this, Socrates, I will tell you.

S: Even someone who was blindfolded would know from your conversation that you are handsome and still have lovers.

M: Why so?

S: Because you are forever giving orders in a discussion, as spoiled people do, who behave like tyrants as long as they are young. And perhaps you have recognized that I am at a disadvantage with handsome people, so I will do you the favour of an answer.

c

M: By all means do me that favour.

S: Do you want me to answer after the manner of Gorgias, which you would most easily follow?

S: Of course I want that.

S: Do you both say there are effluvia of things, as Empedocles[6] does? — Certainly.

S: And that there are channels through which the effluvia make their way? — Definitely.

S: And some effluvia fit some of the channels, while others are too small or too big? — That is so.

d

S: And there is something which you call sight? — There is.

S: From this, "comprehend what I state," as Pindar said, for colour is an effluvium from shapes which fits the sight and is perceived.

M: That

S: Perh   tomed. At
the same ti   sound is,
and smell, a

e

S: It is   than that
about shape

S: It is   the other
is, and I th   before the
mysteries as   ated.

M: I w   these.

77

S: I sh   ich things,
both for yo   you many.

6. Emped   ical philoso-
pher. For hir   ), the inter-
mingling an   e reference
here is to his

7. Theatri   locles and a
quotation fr   s' definition
of shape.

[Handwritten notes:]

Shapes - analogy to explain
virtue? ⤷ follows color

• effluvia

• 76e ◯

• Meno - cannot think for
himself - demands answers -
doesn't know himself

Come now, you too try to fulfill your promise to me and tell me the nature of virtue as a whole and stop making many out of one, as jokers say whenever someone breaks something; but allow virtue to remain whole and sound, and tell me what it is, for I have given you examples.

M: I think, Socrates, that virtue is, as the poet says, "to find joy in beautiful things and have power." So I say that virtue is to desire beautiful things and have the power to acquire them.

S: Do you mean that the man who desires beautiful things desires good things? — Most certainly.

S: Do you assume that there are people who desire bad things, and others who desire good things? Do you not think, my good man, that all men desire good things?

M: I do not.

S: But some desire bad things? — Yes.

S: Do you mean that they believe the bad things to be good, or that they know they are bad and nevertheless desire them? — I think there are both kinds.

S: Do you think, Meno, that anyone, knowing that bad things are bad, nevertheless desires them? — I certainly do.

S: What do you mean by desiring? Is it to secure for oneself? — What else?

S: Does he think that the bad things benefit him who possesses them, or does he know they harm him?

M: There are some who believe that the bad things benefit them, others who know that the bad things harm them.

S: And do you think that those who believe that bad things benefit them know that they are bad?

M: No, that I cannot altogether believe.

S: It is clear then that those who do not know things to be bad do not desire what is bad, but they desire those things that they believe to be good but that are in fact bad. It follows that those who have no knowledge of these things and believe them to be good clearly desire good things. Is that not so? — It is likely.

S: Well then, those who you say desire bad things, believing that bad things harm their possessor, know that they will be harmed by them? — Necessarily.

S: And do they not think that those who are harmed are miserable to the extent that they are harmed? — That too is inevitable.

S: And that those who are miserable are unhappy? — I think so.

b

c

d

e

78

S: Does anyone wish to be miserable and unhappy? — I do not think so, Socrates.

S: No one then wants what is bad, Meno, unless he wants to be such. For what else is being miserable but to desire bad things and secure them?

M: You are probably right, Socrates, and no one wants what is bad.   b

S: Were you not saying just now that virtue is to desire good things and have the power to secure them? — Yes, I was.

S: The desiring part of this statement is common to everybody, and one man is no better man another in this? — So it appears.

S: Clearly then, if one man is better than another, he must be better at securing them. — Quite so.

S: This then is virtue according to your argument, the power of securing good things.   c

M: I think, Socrates, that the case is altogether as you now understand it.

S: Let us see then whether what you say is true, for you may well be right. You say that the capacity to acquire good things is virtue? — I do.

S: And by good things you mean, for example, health and wealth?

M: Yes, and also to acquire gold and silver, also honours and offices in the city.

S: By good things you do not mean other goods than these?

M: No, but I mean all things of this kind.

S: Very well. According to Meno, the hereditary guest friend of the   d Great King, virtue is the acquisition of gold and silver. Do you add to this acquiring, Meno, the words justly and piously, or does it make no difference to you but even if one secures these things unjustly, you call it virtue none the less?

M: Certainly not, Socrates.

S: You would then call it wickedness? — Indeed I would.

S: It seems then that the acquisition must be accompanied by justice or moderation or piety or some other part of virtue; if it is not, it will not be   e virtue, even though it provides good things.

M: How could there be virtue without these?

S: Then failing to secure gold and silver, whenever it would not be just to do so, either for oneself or another, is not this failure to secure them also virtue?

M: So it seems.

S: Then to provide these goods would not be virtue any more than not to provide them, but apparently whatever is done with justice will be virtue,   79 and what is done without anything of the kind is wickedness.

M: I think it must necessarily be as you say.

S: We said a little while ago that each of these things was a part of virtue, namely, justice and moderation and all such things? — Yes.

S: Then you are playing with me, Meno. — How so, Socrates?

S: Because I begged you just now not to break up or fragment virtue, and I gave examples of how you should answer. You paid no attention, but you tell me that virtue is to be able to secure good things with justice, and this, you say, is a part of virtue.

M: I do.

S: It follows then from what you agree to, that to act in whatever you do with a part of virtue is virtue, for you say that justice is a part of virtue, as are all such qualities. Why do I say this? Because when I begged you to tell me about virtue as a whole, you are far from telling me what it is. Rather, you say that every action is virtue if it is performed with a part of virtue, as if you had told me what virtue as a whole is, and I would already know that, even if you fragment it into parts.[8] I think you must face the same question from the beginning, my dear Meno, namely, what is virtue, if every action performed with a part of virtue is virtue? For that is what one is saying when he says that every action performed with justice is virtue. Do you not think you should face the same question again, or do you think one knows what a part of virtue is if one does not know virtue itself? — I do not think so.

S: If you remember, when I was answering you about shape, we rejected the kind of answer that tried to answer in terms still being the subject of inquiry and not yet agreed upon. — And we were right to reject them.

S: Then surely, my good sir, you must not think, while the nature of virtue as a whole is still under inquiry, that by answering in terms of the parts of virtue you can make its nature clear to anyone or make anything else clear by speaking in this way, but only that the same question must be put to you again—what do you take the nature of virtue to be when you say what you say? Or do you think there is no point in what I am saying? — I think what you say is right.

S: Answer me again then from the beginning: What do you and your friend say that virtue is?

M: Socrates, before I even met you I used to hear that you are always in a state of perplexity and that you bring others to the same state, and now I think you are bewitching and beguiling me, simply putting me under a spell, so that I am quite perplexed. Indeed, if a joke is in order, you seem, in appearance and in every other way, to be like the broad torpedo fish, for it too makes anyone who comes close and touches it feel numb, and you now seem to have had that kind of effect on me, for both my mind and my tongue

8. That is, Meno is including the term to be defined in the definition.

are numb, and I have no answer to give you. Yet I have made many speeches about virtue before large audiences on a thousand occasions, very good speeches as I [...] you are
wise not to sa[...] ou were
to behave lik[...] en away
for practising [...]

S: You a[...]

M: Why [...]

S: I kno[...]

M: Why [...]

S: So th[...] w that all
handsome m[...] ntage, for
I think that t[...] will draw
no image of [...] so makes
others numb[...] not have
the answer [...] n anyone
when I cause[...] ue is; perhaps you kn[...] y like one
who does no[...] ether with
you what it [...]

[handwritten note:]
S: asks to define virtue again
M - desire beautiful things + acquire w/ power
↳ "as the poet says" - not
not ↑ his own definition
aporia (80a-b)
↳ not "a way through
↳ translated by perplexity

M: How [...] t all what it is? How will you aim to search for something you do not know at all? If you should meet with it, how will you know that this is the thing that you did not know?

S: I know what you want to say, Meno. Do you realize what a debater's argument you are bringing up, that a man cannot search either for what he knows or for what he does not know? He cannot search for what he knows—since he knows it, there is no need to search—nor for what he does not know, for he does not know what to look for.

M: Does that argument not seem sound to you, Socrates?

S: Not to me.

M: Can you tell me why?

S: I can. I have heard wise men and women talk about divine matters . . .

M: What did they say?

S: What was, I thought, both true and beautiful.

M: What was it, and who were they?

S: The speakers were among the priests and priestesses whose care it is to be able to give an account of their practices. Pindar too says it, and many others of the divine among our poets. What they say is this; see whether you think they speak the truth: They say that the human soul is immortal; at times it comes to an end, which they call dying, at times it is reborn, but it is never destroyed, and one must therefore live one's life as piously as possible:

> *Persephone will return to the sun above in the ninth year*
> *the souls of those from whom*
> *she will exact punishment for old miseries,*
> *and from these come noble kings,*
> *mighty in strength and greatest in wisdom,*
> *and for the rest of time men will call them sacred heroes.*

c

As the soul is immortal, has been born often and has seen all things here and in the underworld, there is nothing which it has not learned; so it is in no way surprising that it can recollect the things it knew before, both about virtue and other things. As the whole of nature is akin, and the soul has learned everything, nothing prevents a man, after recalling one thing only—a process men call learning—discovering everything else for himself, if he is brave and does not tire of the search, for searching and learning are, as a whole, recollection. We must, therefore, not believe that debater's argument, for it would make us idle, and fainthearted men like to hear it, whereas my argument makes them energetic and keen on the search. I trust that this is true, and I want to inquire along with you into the nature of virtue.

d

e

M: Yes, Socrates, but how do you mean that we do not learn, but that what we call learning is recollection? Can you teach me that this is so?

S: As I said just now, Meno, you are a rascal. You now ask me if I can teach you, when I say there is no teaching but recollection, in order to show me up at once as contradicting myself.

82

M: No, by Zeus, Socrates, that was not my intention when I spoke, but just a habit. If you can somehow show me that things are as you say, please do so.

S: It is not easy, but I am nevertheless willing to do my best for your sake. Call one of these many attendants of yours, whichever you like, that I may prove it to you in his case.

b

M: Certainly. You there, come forward.

S: Is he a Greek? Does he speak Greek?

M: Very much so. He was born in my household.

S: Pay attention then whether you think he is recollecting or learning from me.

M: I will pay attention.

S: Tell me now, boy, you know that a square figure is like this? — I do.

S: A square then is a figure in which all these four sides are equal? — Yes indeed.

c

S: And it also has these lines through the middle equal?[9] — Yes.

S: And such a figure could be larger or smaller? — Certainly.

S: If then this side were two feet, and this other side two feet, how many feet would the whole be? Consider it this way: if it were two feet this way, and only one foot that way, the figure[10] would be once two feet? — Yes.

S: But if it is two feet also that way, it would surely be twice two feet? —   d Yes.

S: How many feet is twice two feet? Work it out and tell me. — Four, Socrates.

S: Now we could have another figure twice the size of this one, with the four sides equal like this one. — Yes.

S: How many feet will that be? — Eight.

S: Come now, try to tell me how long each side of this will be. The side of this is two feet. What about each side of the one which is its   e double? — Obviously, Socrates, it will be twice the length.

S: You see, Meno, that I am not teaching the boy anything, but all I do is question him. And now he thinks he knows the length of the line on which an eight-foot figure is based. Do you agree? — I do.

_____

9. Socrates draws a square ABCD. The sides are of course equal, and the "lines through the middle" are the line joining the middle points of these sides, which also go through the center of the square, namely EF and GH.

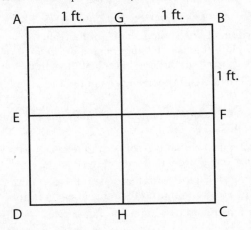

He then goes on to asume the sides to be two feet.

10. I.e., the rectangle ABFE, which is obviously two square feet.

S: And does he know? — Certainly not.

S: He thinks it is a line twice the length? — Yes.

S: Watch him now recollecting things in order, as one must recollect. Tell me, boy, do you say that a figure double the size is based on a line double the length? Now I mean such a figure as this, not long on one side and short on the other, but equal in every direction like this one, and double the size, that is, eight feet. See whether you still believe that it will be based on a line double the length. — I do.

S: Now the line becomes double its length if we add another of the same length here? — Yes indeed.

S: And the eight-foot square will be based on it, if there are four lines of that length? — Yes.

S: Well, let us draw from it four equal lines, and surely that is what you say is the eight-foot square? — Certainly.

S: And within this figure are four squares, each of which is equal to the four-foot square? — Yes.

S: How big is it then? Is it not four times as big? — Of course.

S: Is this square then, which is four times as big, its double? — No, by Zeus.

S: How many times bigger is it? — Four times.

S: Then, my boy, the figure based on a line twice the length is not double but four times as big? — You are right.

S: And four times four is sixteen, is it not? — Yes.

S: On how long a line should the eight-foot square be based? On *this* line we have a square that is four times bigger, do we not? — Yes. Now this four-foot square is based on this line here, half the length? — Yes.

S: Very well. Is the eight-foot square not double this one and half that one?[11] — Yes.

S: Will it not be based on a line longer than this one and shorter than that one? Is that not so? — I think so.

S: Good, you answer what you think. And tell me, was this one not two-feet long, and that one four feet? — Yes.

S: The line on which the eight-foot square is based must then be longer than this one of two feet, and shorter than that one of four feet? — It must be.

S: Try to tell me then how long a line you say it is. — Three feet.

---

11. I.e., the eight-foot square is double the four-foot square and half the sixteen-foot square, double the square based on a line two-feet long, and half the square based on a four-foot side, so it must be based on a line between two and four feet in length. The slave naturally suggests three feet, but that gives a nine-foot square, and is still wrong (83e).

Margin markers: 83, b, c, d, e

S: Then if it is three feet, let us add the half of this one, and it will be three feet? For these are two feet, and the other is one. And here, similarly, these are two feet and that one is one foot, and so the figure you mention comes to be? — Yes.

S: Now if it is three feet this way and three feet that way, will the whole figure be three times three feet? — So it seems.

S: How much is three times three feet? — Nine feet.

S: And the double square was to be how many feet? — Eight.

S: So the eight-foot figure cannot be based on the three-foot line? — Clearly not.

S: But on how long a line? Try to tell us exactly, and if you do not want   84
to work it out, show me from what line. — By Zeus, Socrates, I do not know.

S: You realize, Meno, what point he has reached in his recollection. At first he did not know what the basic line of the eight-foot square was; even now he does not yet know, but then he thought he knew, and answered confidently as if he did know, and he did not think himself at a loss, but now he does think himself at a loss, and as he does not know, neither does he think   b
he knows. — That is true.

S: So he is now in a better position with regard to the matter he does not know?

M: I agree with that too.

S: Have we done him any harm by making him perplexed and numb as the torpedo fish does? — I do not think so.

S: Indeed, we have probably achieved something relevant to finding out how matters stand, for now, as he does not know, he would be glad to find out, whereas before he thought he could easily make many fine speeches to large audiences about the square of double size and said that it   c
must have a base twice as long. — So it seems.

S: Do you think that before he would have tried to find out that which he thought he knew though he did not, before he fell into perplexity and realized he did not know and longed to know? — I do not think so, Socrates.

S: Has he then benefitted from being numbed? — I think so.

S: Look then how he will come out of his perplexity while searching along with me. I shall do nothing more than ask questions and not teach him. Watch whether you find me teaching and explaining things to him   d
instead of asking for his opinion.

S: You tell me, is this not a four-foot figure? You understand? — I do.

S: We add to it this figure which is equal to it? — Yes.

S: And we add this third figure equal to each of them? — Yes.

S: Could we then fill in the space in the corner? — Certainly.[12]

S: So we have these four equal figures? — Yes.

e   S: Well then, how many times is the whole figure larger than this one?[13] — Four times.

S: But we should have had one that was twice as large, or do you not remember? — I certainly do.

85   S: Does not this line from one corner to the other cut each of these figures in two?[14] — Yes.

---

12. Socrates now builds up his sixteen-foot square by joining two four-foot squares, then a third, like this:

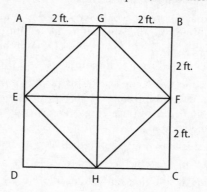

Filling "the space in the corner" will give another four-foot square, which completes the sixteen-foot square containing four four-foot squares.

13. "This one" is any one of the inside squares of four feet.

14. Socrates now draws the diagonals of the four inside squares, namely, FH, HE, EG and GF, which together form the square GFHEG. We should note that Socrates here introduces a new element, which is not the result of a question but of his own knowledge, though the answer to the problem follows from questions. The new square contains four halves of a four-foot square, and is therefore eight feet.

S: So these are four equal lines which enclose this figure? — They are.

S: Consider now: how large is the figure? — I do not understand.

S: Within these four figures, each line cuts off half of each, does it not?
— Yes.

S: How many of this size are there in this figure? — Four.

S: How many in this? — Two.

S: What is the relation of four to two? — Double.   b

S: How many feet in this? — Eight.

S: Based on what line? — This one.

S: That is, on the line that stretches from corner to corner of the four-
foot figure? — Yes. — Clever men call this the diagonal, so that if diagonal
is its name, you say that the double figure would be that based on the diagonal? — Most certainly, Socrates.

S: What do you think, Meno? Has he, in his answers, expressed any
opinion that was not his own?   c

M: No, they were all his own.

S: And yet, as we said a short time ago, he did not know? — That is
true.

S: So these opinions were in him, were they not? — Yes.

S: So the man who does not know has within himself true opinions
about the things that he does not know? — So it appears.

S: These opinions have now just been stirred up like a dream, but if
he were repeatedly asked these same questions in various ways, you know
that in the end his knowledge about these things would be as accurate as   d
anyone's. — It is likely.

S: And he will know it without having been taught but only questioned,
and find the knowledge within himself? — Yes.

S: And is not finding knowledge within oneself recollection? — Certainly.

S: Must he not either have at some time acquired the knowledge he
now possesses, or else have always possessed it? — Yes.

S: If he always had it, he would always have known. If he acquired
it, he cannot have done so in his present life. Or has someone taught him   e
geometry? For he will perform in the same way about all geometry, and all
other knowledge. Has someone taught him everything? You should know,
especially as he has been born and brought up in your house.

M: But I know that no one has taught him.

S: Yet he has these opinions, or doesn't he?

M: That seems indisputable, Socrates.

86   S: If he has not acquired them in his present life, is it not clear that he had them and had learned them at some other time? — It seems so.

S: Then that was the time when he was not a human being? — Yes.

S: If then, during the time he exists and is not a human being he will have true opinions which, when stirred by questioning, become knowledge, will not his soul have learned during all time? For it is clear that during all time he exists, either as a man or not. — So it seems.

b   S: Then if the truth about reality is always in our soul, the soul would be immortal so that you should always confidently try to seek out and recollect what you do not know at present—that is, what you do not recollect?[15]

M: Somehow, Socrates, I think that what you say is right.

S: I think so too, Meno. I do not insist that my argument is right in all other respects, but I would contend at all costs both in word and deed as far as I could that we will be better men, braver and less idle, if we believe that one must search for the things one does not know, rather than if we believe

c   that it is not possible to find out what we do not know and that we must not look for it.

M: In this too I think you are right, Socrates.

S: Since we are of one mind that one should seek to find out what one does not know, shall we try to find out together what virtue is?

M: Certainly. But Socrates, I should be most pleased to investigate and hear your answer to my original question, whether we should try on the

d   assumption that virtue is something teachable, or is a natural gift, or in whatever way it comes to men.

S: If I were directing you, Meno, and not only myself, we would not have investigated whether virtue is teachable or not before we had investigated what virtue itself is. But because you do not even attempt to rule yourself, in order that you may be free, but you try to rule me and do so, I will agree with you—for what can I do? So we must, it appears, inquire into the

e   qualities of something the nature of which we do not yet know. However, please relax your rule a little bit for me and agree to investigate whether it is teachable or not by means of a hypothesis. I mean the way geometers often carry on their investigations. For example, if they are asked whether a

87   specific area can be inscribed in the form of a triangle within a given circle, one of them might say: "I do not yet know whether that area has that property, but I think I have, as it were, a hypothesis that is of use for the problem, namely this: If that area is such that when one has applied it as a rectangle to the given straight line in the circle it is deficient by a fig-

b   ure similar to the very figure which is applied, then I think one alternative results, whereas another results if it is impossible for this to happen. So, by using this hypothesis, I am willing to tell you what results with

---

15. This is what the whole passage on recollection with the slave is intended to prove, namely, that the sophism introduced by Meno—that one cannot find out what one does not know—is false.

regard to inscribing it in the circle—that is, whether it is impossible or not."* So let us speak about virtue also, since we do not know either what it is or what qualities it possesses, and let us investigate whether it is teachable or not by means of a hypothesis, and say this: Among the things existing in the soul, of what sort is virtue, that it should be teachable or not? First, if it is another sort than knowledge, is it teachable or not, as we were just saying, recollectable? Let it make no difference to us which c term we use: is it teachable? Or is it plain to anyone that men cannot be taught anything but knowledge? — I think so.

S: But, if virtue is a kind of knowledge, it is clear that it could be taught. — Of course.

S: We have dealt with that question quickly, that if it is of one kind it can be taught, if it is of a different kind, it cannot. — We have indeed.

S: The next point to consider seems to be whether virtue is knowledge or something else. — That does seem to be the next point to consider. d

S: Well now, do we say that virtue is itself something good, and will this hypothesis stand firm for us, that it is something good? — Of course.

S: If then there is anything else good that is different and separate from knowledge, virtue might well not be a kind of knowledge; but if there is nothing good that knowledge does not encompass, we would be right to suspect that it is a kind of knowledge. — That is so.

S: Surely virtue makes us good? — Yes. e

S: And if we are good, we are beneficent, for all that is good is beneficial. Is that not so? — Yes.

S: So virtue is something beneficial?

M: That necessarily follows from what has been agreed.

S: Let us then examine what kinds of things benefit us, taking them up one by one: health, we say, and strength, and beauty, and also wealth. We say that these things, and others of the same kind, benefit us, do we not? — We do.

S: Yet we say that these same things also sometimes harm one. Do you 88 agree or not? — I do.

S: Look then, what directing factor determines in each case whether these things benefit or harm us? Is it not the right use of them that benefits us, and the wrong use that harms us? — Certainly.

S: Let us now look at the qualities of the soul. There is something you call moderation, and justice, courage, intelligence, memory, munificence, and all such things? — There is.

S: Consider whichever of these you believe not to be knowledge but b different from it; do they not at times harm us, at other times benefit us? Courage, for example, when it is not wisdom but like a kind of reckless-

*The translation here follows the interpretation of T.L. Heath, *A History of Greek Mathematics* (Oxford: Clarendon Press, 1921), vol. I pp. 298 ff.

ness: when a man is reckless without understanding, he is harmed, when with understanding, he is benefitted. — Yes.

S: The same is true of moderation and mental quickness; when they are learned and disciplined with understanding they are beneficial, but without understanding they are harmful? — Very much so.

c   S: Therefore, in a word, all that the soul undertakes and endures, if directed by wisdom, ends in happiness, but if directed by ignorance, it ends in the opposite? — That is likely.

S: If then virtue is something in the soul and it must be beneficial, it must be knowledge, since all the qualities of the soul are in themselves

d   neither beneficial nor harmful, but accompanied by wisdom or folly they become harmful or beneficial. This argument shows that virtue, being beneficial, must be a kind of wisdom. — I agree.

S: Furthermore, those other things we were mentioning just now, wealth and the like, are at times good and at times harmful. Just as for the rest of the soul the direction of wisdom makes things beneficial, but

e   harmful if directed by folly, so in these cases, if the soul uses and directs them right it makes them beneficial, but bad use makes them harmful? — Quite so.

S: The wise soul directs them right, the foolish soul wrongly? — That is so.

S: So one may say this about everything: all other human activities depend on the soul, and those of the soul itself depend on wisdom if they

89   are to be good. According to this argument the beneficial would be wisdom, and we say that virtue is beneficial? — Certainly.

S: Virtue then, as a whole or in part, is wisdom?

M: What you say, Socrates, seems to me quite right.

S: Then, if that is so, the good are not so by nature? — I do not think they are.

b   S: For if they were, this would follow: if the good were so by nature, we would have people who knew which among the young were by nature good; we would take those whom they had pointed out and guard them in the Acropolis, sealing them up there much more carefully than gold so that no one could corrupt them, and when they reached maturity they would be useful to their cities. — Reasonable enough, Socrates.

c   S: Since the good are not good by nature, does learning make them so?

M: Necessarily, as I now think, Socrates, and clearly, on our hypothesis, if virtue is knowledge, it can be taught.

S: Perhaps, by Zeus, but may it be that we were not right to agree to this?

M: Yet it seemed to be right at the time.

S: We should not only think it right at the time, but also now and in the future if it is to be at all sound.

M: What is the difficulty? What do you have in mind that you do not   d
like about it and doubt that virtue is knowledge?

S: I will tell you, Meno. I am not saying that it is wrong to say that virtue is teachable if it is knowledge, but look whether it is reasonable of me to doubt whether it is knowledge. Tell me this: if not only virtue but anything whatever can be taught, should there not be of necessity people who teach it and people who learn it? — I think so.

S: Then again, if on the contrary there are no teachers or learners of   e
something, we should be right to assume that the subject cannot be taught?

M: Quite so, but do you think that there are no teachers of virtue?

S: I have often tried to find out whether there were any teachers of it, but in spite of all my efforts I cannot find any. And yet I have searched for them with the help of many people, especially those whom I believed to be most experienced in this matter. And now, Meno, Anytus[16] here has opportunely come to sit down by us. Let us share our search with him. It would be reasonable for us to do so, for Anytus, in the first place, is the son of   90
Anthemion, a man of wealth and wisdom, who did not become rich automatically or as the result of a gift like Ismenias the Theban, who recently acquired the possessions of Polycrates, but through his own wisdom and efforts. Further, he did not seem to be an arrogant or puffed up or offensive citizen in other ways, but he was a well-mannered and well-behaved man. Also he gave our friend here a good upbringing and education, as the   b
majority of Athenians believe, for they are electing him to the highest offices. It is right then to look for the teachers of virtue with the help of men such as he, whether there are any and if so who they are. Therefore, Anytus, please join me and your guest friend Meno here, in our inquiry as to who are the teachers of virtue. Look at it in this way: if we wanted Meno to become a good physician, to what teachers would we send him? Would we not   c
send him to the physicians? — Certainly.

S: And if we wanted him to be a good shoemaker, to shoemakers? —
Yes.

S: And so with other pursuits? — Certainly.

S: Tell me again on this same topic, like this: we say that we would be right to send him to the physicians if we want him to become a physician; whenever we say that, we mean that it would be reasonable to send him to   d
those who practise the craft rather than to those who do not, and to those who exact fees for this very practice and have shown themselves to be teachers of anyone who wishes to come to them and learn. Is it not with this in mind that we would be right to send him? — Yes.

---

16. For Anytus, see Introduction, p. 1.

S: And the same is true about flute-playing and the other crafts? It would be very foolish for those who want to make someone a flute-player to refuse to send him to those who profess to teach the craft and make money at it, but to send him to make trouble for others by seeking to learn from those who do not claim to be teachers or have a single pupil in that subject which we want the one we send to learn from them? Do you not think it very unreasonable to do so? — By Zeus I do, and also very ignorant.

S: Quite right. However, you can now deliberate with me about our guest friend Meno here. He has been telling me for some time, Anytus, that he longs to acquire that wisdom and virtue which enables men to manage their households and their cities well, to take care of their parents, to know how to welcome and to send away both citizens and strangers as a good man should. Consider to whom we should be right to send him to learn this virtue. Or is it obvious in view of what was said just now that we should send him to those who profess to be teachers of virtue and have shown themselves to be available to any Greek who wishes to learn, and for this fix a fee and exact it?

A: And who do you say these are, Socrates?

S: You surely know yourself that they are those whom men call sophists.

A: By Heracles, hush, Socrates. May no one of my household or friends, whether citizen or stranger, be mad enough to go to these people and be harmed by them, for they clearly cause the ruin and corruption of their followers.

S: How do you mean, Anytus? Are these people, alone of those who claim the knowledge to benefit one, so different from the others that they not only do not benefit what one entrusts to them but on the contrary corrupt it, even though they obviously expect to make money from the process? I find I cannot believe you, for I know that one man, Protagoras, made more money from this knowledge of his than Phidias who made such notably fine works, and ten other sculptors. Surely what you say is extraordinary, if those who mend old sandals and restore clothes would be found out within the month if they returned the clothes and sandals in a worse state than they received them; if they did this they would soon die of starvation, but the whole of Greece has not noticed for forty years that Protagoras corrupts those who frequent him and sends them away in a worse moral condition than he received them. I believe that he was nearly seventy when he died and had practised his craft for forty years. During all that time to this very day his reputation has stood high; and not only Protagoras but a great many others, some born before him and some still alive today. Are we to say that you maintain that they deceive and harm the young knowingly, or that they themselves are not aware of it? Are we to deem those whom some people consider the wisest of men to be so mad as that?

A: They are far from being mad, Socrates. It is much rather those among the young who pay their fees who are mad, and even more the relatives who entrust their young to them and most of all the cities who allow   b them to come in and do not drive out any citizen or stranger who attempts to behave in this manner.

S: Has some sophist wronged you, Anytus, or why are you so hard on them?

A: No, by Zeus, I have never met one of them, nor would I allow any one of my people to do so.

S: Are you then altogether without any experience of these men?

A: And may I remain so.

S: How then, my good sir, can you know whether there is any good in   c their instruction or not, if you are altogether without experience of it?

A: Easily, for I know who they are, whether I have experience of them or not.

S: Perhaps you are a wizard, Anytus, for I wonder, from what you yourself say, how else you know about these things. However, let us not try to find out who the men are whose company would make Meno wicked—let   d them be the sophists if you like—but tell us, and benefit your family friend here by telling him, to whom he should go in so large a city to acquire, to any worthwhile degree, the virtue I was just now describing.

A: Why did you not tell him yourself?

S: I did mention those whom I thought to be teachers of it, but you say I am wrong, and perhaps you are right. You tell him in your turn to whom   e among the Athenians he should go. Tell him the name of anyone you want.

A: Why give him the name of one individual? Any Athenian gentleman he may meet, if he is willing to be persuaded, will make him a better man than the sophists would.

S: And have these gentlemen become virtuous automatically, without learning from anyone, and are they able to teach others what they them-   93 selves never learned?

A: I believe that these men have learned from those who were gentlemen before them; or do you not think that there are many good men in this city?

S: I believe, Anytus, that there are many men here who are good at public affairs, and that there have been as many in the past, but have they been good teachers of their own virtue? That is the point we are discussing, not whether there are good men here or not, or whether there have been in b the past, but we have been investigating for some time whether virtue can be taught. And in the course of that investigation we are inquiring whether the good men of today and of the past knew how to pass on to another the virtue they themselves possessed, or whether a man cannot pass it on or receive it from another. This is what Meno and I have been investigating for some

c time. Look at it this way, from what you yourself have said. Would you not say that Themistocles was a good man? — Yes. Even the best of men.

S: And therefore a good teacher of his own virtue if anyone was?

A: I think so, if he wanted to be.

S: But do you think he did not want some other people to be worthy men, and especially his own son? Or do you think he begrudged him this,

d and deliberately did not pass on to him his own virtue? Have you not heard that Themistocles taught his son Cleophantus to be a good horseman? He could remain standing upright on horseback and shoot javelins from that position and do many other remarkable things which his father had him taught and made skillful at, all of which required good teachers. Have you not heard this from your elders? — I have.

S: So one could not blame the poor natural talents of the son for his

e failure in virtue? — Perhaps not.

S: But have you ever heard anyone, young or old, say that Cleophantus, the son of Themistocles, was a good and wise man at the same pursuits as his father? — Never.

S: Are we to believe that he wanted to educate his son in those other things but not to do better than his neighbors in that skill which he himself possessed, if indeed virtue can be taught? — Perhaps not, by Zeus.

S: And yet he was, as you yourself agree, among the best teachers

94 of virtue in the past. Let us consider another man, Aristides, the son of Lysimachus. Do you not agree that he was good? — I very definitely do.

S: He too gave his own son Lysimachus the best Athenian education in matters which are the business of teachers, and do you think he made him a better man than anyone else? For you have been in his company and

b seen the kind of man he is. Or take Pericles, a man of such magnificent wisdom. You know that he brought up two sons, Paralus and Xanthippus? — I know.

S: You also know that he taught them to be as good horsemen as any Athenian, that he educated them in the arts, in gymnastics, and in all else that was a matter of skill not to be inferior to anyone, but did he not want to make them good men? I think he did, but this could not be taught. And lest you think that only a few most inferior Athenians are incapable in this

respect, reflect that Thucydides[17] too brought up two sons, Melesias and   c
Stephanus, that he educated them well in all other things. They were the
best wrestlers in Athens—he entrusted the one to Xanthias and the other
to Eudorus, who were thought to be the best wrestlers of the day, or do you
not remember?

A: I remember I have heard that said.

S: It is surely clear that he would not have taught his boys what it costs   d
money to teach, but have failed to teach them what costs nothing—making
them good men—if that could be taught? Or was Thucydides perhaps an
inferior person who had not many friends among the Athenians and the
allies? He belonged to a great house; he had great influence in the city and
among the other Greeks, so that if virtue could be taught he would have
found the man who could make his sons good men, be it a citizen or a
stranger, if he himself did not have the time because of his public concerns.   e
But, friend Anytus, virtue can certainly not be taught.

A: I think, Socrates, that you easily speak ill of people. I would advise
you, if you will listen to me, to be careful. Perhaps also in another city, and
certainly here, it is easier to injure people than to benefit them. I think you
know that yourself.   95

S: I think, Meno, that Anytus is angry, and I am not at all surprised.
He thinks, to begin with, that I am slandering those men, and then he
believes himself to be one of them. If he ever realizes what slander is, he will
cease from anger, but he does not know it now. You tell me, are there not
worthy men among your people? — Certainly.

S: Well now, are they willing to offer themselves to the young as teach-   b
ers? Do they agree they are teachers, and that virtue can be taught?

M: No, by Zeus, Socrates, but sometimes you would hear them say that
it can be taught, at other times, that it cannot.

S: Should we say that they are teachers of this subject, when they do
not even agree on this point? — I do not think so, Socrates.

S: Further, do you think that these sophists, who alone profess to be so,
are teachers of virtue?

M: I admire this most in Gorgias, Socrates, that you would never hear   c
him promising this. Indeed, he ridicules the others when he hears them
making this claim. He thinks one should make people clever speakers.

S: You do not think then that the sophists are teachers?

M: I cannot tell, Socrates; like most people, at times I think they are, at
other times I think that they are not.

---

17. Not the historian but Thucydides the son of Melesias, an Athenin statesman who
was an opponent of Pericles and who was ostracized in 440 B.C.

d S: Do you know that not only you and the other public men at times think that it can be taught, at other times that it cannot, but that the poet Theognis[18] says the same thing? — Where?

S: In his elegiacs: "Eat and drink with these men, and keep their company. Please those whose power is great, for you will learn goodness from the good. If you mingle with bad men you will lose even what wit you possess." You see that here he speaks as if virtue can be taught? — So it appears.

S: Elsewhere, he changes somewhat: "if this could be done" he says, "and intelligence could be instilled," somehow those who could do this "would collect large and numerous fees," and further: "Never would a bad son be born of a good father, for he would be persuaded by wise words, but you will never make a bad man good by teaching." You realize that the poet is contradicting himself on the same subject? — He seems to be.

S: Can you mention any other subject of which those who claim to be teachers not only are not recognized to be teachers of others but are not recognized to have knowledge of it themselves, and are thought to be poor in the very matter which they profess to teach? Or any other subject of which those who are recognized as worthy teachers at one time say it can be taught and at other times that it cannot? Would you say that people who are so confused about a subject can be effective teachers of it? — No, by Zeus, I would not.

S: If then neither the sophists nor the worthy people themselves are teachers of this subject, clearly there would be no others? — I do not think there are.

c S: If there are no teachers, neither are there pupils? — As you say.

S: And we agreed that a subject that has neither teachers nor pupils is not teachable? — We have so agreed.

S: Now there seem to be no teachers of virtue anywhere? — That is so.

S: If there are no teachers, there are no learners? — That seems so.

S: Then virtue cannot be taught?

d M: Apparently not, if we have investigated this correctly. I certainly wonder, Socrates, whether there are no good men either, or in what way good men come to be.

S: We are probably poor specimens, you and I, Meno. Gorgias has not adequately educated you, nor Prodicus me. We must then at all costs turn our attention to ourselves and find someone who will in some way make us e better. I say this in view of our recent investigation, for it is ridiculous that we failed to see that it is not only under the guidance of knowledge that men

---

18. Theognis was a poet of mid-sixth century B.C. A collection of poems is extant (about twelve hundred lines), but the authenticity of a good deal of it is doubtful.

succeed in their affairs, and that is perhaps why the knowledge of how good men come to be escapes us.

M: How do you mean, Socrates?

S: I mean this: we were right to agree that good men must be benefi-cent, and that this could not be otherwise. Is that not so? — Yes.

S: And that they will be beneficent if they give us correct guidance in our affairs. To this too we were right to agree? — Yes.   97

S: But that one cannot guide correctly if one does not have knowledge; to this our agreement is likely to be incorrect. — How do you mean?

S: I will tell you. A man who knew the way to Larissa, or anywhere else you like, and went there and guided others would surely lead them well and correctly? — Certainly.

S: What if someone had had a correct opinion as to which was the way   b but had not gone there nor indeed had knowledge of it, would he not also lead correctly? — Certainly.

S: And as long as he has the right opinion about that of which the other has knowledge, he will not be a worse guide than the one who knows, as he has a true opinion, though not knowledge. — In no way worse.

S: So true opinion is in no way a worse guide to correct action than knowledge. It is this that we omitted in our investigation of the nature of virtue, when we said that only knowledge can lead to correct action, for true   c opinion can do so also. — So it seems.

S: So correct opinion is no less useful than knowledge?

M: Yes, to this extent, Socrates. But the man who has knowledge will always succeed, whereas he who has true opinion will only succeed at times.

S: How do you mean? Will he who has the right opinion not always succeed, as long as his opinion is right?

M: That appears to be so of necessity, and it makes me wonder, Socrates, this being the case, why knowledge is prized far more highly than   d right opinion, and why they are different.

S: Do you know why you wonder, or shall I tell you? — By all means tell me.

S: It is because you have paid no attention to the statues of Daedalus, but perhaps there are none in Thessaly.

M: What do you have in mind when you say this?

S: That they too run away and escape if one does not tie them down but remain in place if tied down. — So what?   e

S: To acquire an untied work of Daedalus is not worth much, like acquiring a runaway slave, for it does not remain, but it is worth much if tied down, for his works are very beautiful. What am I thinking of when I say this? True opinions. For true opinions, as long as they remain, are a fine thing and all they do is good, but they are not willing to remain long, and they escape from a man's mind, so that they are not worth much until one ties them down by (giving) an account of the reason why. And that, Meno my friend, is recollection, as we previously agreed. After they are tied down, in the first place they become knowledge, and then they remain in place. That is why knowledge is prized higher than correct opinion, and knowledge differs from correct opinion in being tied down.

M: Yes, by Zeus, Socrates, it seems to be something like that.

S: Indeed, I too speak as one who does not have knowledge but is guessing. However, I certainly do not think I am guessing that right opinion is a different thing from knowledge. If I claim to know anything else—and I would make that claim about few things—I would put this down as one of the things I know. — Rightly so, Socrates.

S: Well then, is it not correct that when true opinion guides the course of every action, it does no worse than knowledge? — I think you are right in this too.

S: Correct opinion is then neither inferior to knowledge nor less useful in directing actions, nor is the man who has it less so than he who has knowledge. — That is so.

S: And we agreed that the good man is beneficent. — Yes.

S: Since then it is not only through knowledge but also through right opinion that men are good, and beneficial to their cities when they are, and neither knowledge nor true opinion come to men by nature but are acquired—or do you think either of these comes by nature? — I do not think so.

S: Then if they do not come by nature, men are not so by nature either. — Surely not.

S: As goodness does not come by nature, we inquired next whether it could be taught. — Yes.

S: We thought it could be taught, if it was knowledge? — Yes.

S: And that it was knowledge if it could be taught? — Quite so.

S: And that if there were teachers of it, it could be taught, but if there were not, it was not teachable? — That is so.

S: And then we agreed that there were no teachers of it? — We did.

S: So we agreed that it was neither teachable nor knowledge? — Quite so.

S: But we certainly agree that virtue is a good thing? — Yes.

S: And that which guides correctly is both useful and good? — Certainly.

S: And that only these two things, true belief and knowledge, guide   99
correctly, and that if a man possesses these he gives correct guidance. The
things that turn out right by some chance are not due to human guidance,
but where there is correct human guidance it is due to two things, true belief
or knowledge. — I think that is so.

S: Now because it cannot be taught, virtue no longer seems to be
knowledge? — It seems not.

S: So one of the two good and useful things has been excluded, and   b
knowledge is not the guide in public affairs. — I do not think so.

S: So it is not by some kind of wisdom, or by being wise, that such men
lead their cities, those such as Themistocles and those mentioned by Anytus
just now? That is the reason why they cannot make others be like themselves, because it is not knowledge which makes them what they are.

M: It is likely to be as you say, Socrates.

S: Therefore, if it is not through knowledge, the only alternative is
that it is through right opinion that statesmen follow the right course for   c
their cities. As regards knowledge, they are no different from soothsayers
and prophets. They too say many true things when inspired, but they have
no knowledge of what they are saying. — That is probably so.

S: And so, Meno, is it right to call divine these men who, without any
understanding, are right in much that is of importance in what they say and
do? — Certainly.

S: We should be right to call divine also those soothsayers and prophets whom we just mentioned, and all the poets, and we should call no less   d
divine and inspired those public men who are no less under the gods' influence and possession, as their speeches lead to success in many important
matters, though they have no knowledge of what they are saying. — Quite
so.

S: Women too, Meno, call good men divine, and the Spartans, when
they eulogize someone, say "This man is divine."

M: And they appear to be right, Socrates, though perhaps Anytus here   e
will be annoyed with you for saying so.

S: I do not mind that; we shall talk to him again, but if we were right
in the way in which we spoke and investigated in this whole discussion, virtue would be neither an inborn quality nor taught, but comes to those who
possess it as a gift from the gods which is not accompanied by understanding, unless there is someone among our statesmen who can make another   100

into a statesman. If there were one, he could be said to be among the living as Homer said Teiresias was among the dead, namely, that "he alone retained his wits while the others flitted about like shadows." In the same manner such a man would, as far as virtue is concerned, here also be the only true reality compared, as it were, with shadows.

b   M: I think that is an excellent way to put it, Socrates.

S: It follows from this reasoning, Meno, that virtue appears to be present in those of us who may possess it as a gift from the gods. We shall have clear knowledge of this when, before we investigate how it comes to be present in men, we first try to find out what virtue in itself is. But now the time has come for me to go. You convince your guest friend Anytus here of these very things of which you have yourself been convinced, in order that he may be more amenable. If you succeed, you will also confer a benefit upon the Athenians.

SELECTED BIBLIOGRAPHY

Edition

Plato's Meno. Ed. R. S. Bluck. Cambridge: Cambridge University Press, 1961. Greek text and long introduction and notes.

Secondary Works

Crombie, I. M. *An Examination of Plato's Doctrines.* Vol. 1, *Plato on Knowledge and Reality.* New York: The Humanities Press, 1963.

Guthrie, W. K. C. *A History of Greek Philosophy.* Vols. 3, 4. Cambridge: Cambridge University Press, 1969, 1975.

Klein, Jacob. *A Commentary on Plato's Meno.* Chapel Hill: University of North Carolina Press, 1965.

Raven, J. E. *Plato's Thought in the Making.* Cambridge: Cambridge University Press, 1965. (Chap. 5, "Meno," pp. 56–70.)

Vlastos, Gregory. "*Anamnesis* in the *Meno*," Dialogue, IV (1965), 143–167.

White, Nicholas P. *Plato on Knowledge and Reality.* Indianapolis: Hackett Publishing Company, Inc., 1976. (Chap. II, "The *Meno*: Inquiry and Its Goals," pp. 35–62.)